AF316653

Feudalistic System In 21ˢᵗ Century

Sofia Laurden-Davis Adams

Sofia L. Adams

Copyright © 2024

All Rights Reserved

Dedication

This book is dedicated to people who continue and share good morals, positivity, good commons sense, good wisdom and good conscience to the society. To guide our children to the right path of living on this earth of abundance, plenty, and mixed of good and evil. I am thankful for people who bought this book of mine. Our destination here on earth of abundance and plenty with mixed good and evil is temporary. Therefore, we focus on walking through the right path for good and healthy harvest.

Sofia L. Adams

Acknowledgment

The King will not be able to own me because I will run away. I can live in a small house, a home free of mortgage, utility bills, and other unnecessary expenses. I've heard people say that they would like to live in a big house and so on and come to find out the expenses will kill their cash flow and make holes in their pockets. Truly, by paying a mortgage on your house, insurance, and other expenses, a homeowner becomes a slave of the industries of mortgage, insurance, utility, and construction for renovation and house maintenance.

Unless we are smart enough to earn its cash flow from the house, we are living; therefore, let the tenant pay your mortgage and other expenses in our house. I understand that our freedom to occupy the entire house just for ourselves is diminished. Shall we be rather a slave to the mortgage, insurance, and home maintenance industries? Is it worth it? Does it? Is it because of the pride of having a big house with a white picket fence? Are the huge expenses we shoulder every month worth it? How do we accept the existing pro-humans in our society?

Thinking critically is necessary to be aware of what you are paying. Some say we are not so smart. Perhaps we do not have to think clearly due to our busyness in life such as work and other life responsibility. We just go for it and buy it or sign it without thinking and reading what we are signing for. Our wants completed. Therefore, we think we don't need to go through hardship in life because of our stupidity, pride, and ignorance. Thus, we are smart enough to pay attention to what we are paying. If we search, think, and analyze our hard work, money not only goes to the mortgage, insurance, utilities, and home maintenance industries, but also thrown away.

Although businesses will go down the line, that affects the economy overall, but you as an individual will survive if you know how to carefully manage your financial. In addition, as a person with a smart thinking about financial we will not have a huge debt to struggle to pay for our huge house with all the bills and expenses we cannot afford or work so hard to afford. Balance is the key. The questions are: Are you earning enough money to make a hole in your pocket and be a slave of mortgage, insurance, utility companies, and renovation construction industries? Well, if you can afford all unnecessary expenses, good luck and enjoy your life being a slave to these companies. However, will Artificial Intelligence (AI) take over our debt in the future?

Sofia L. Adams

Table of Contents

INTRODUCTION

In today's era, we are very independent from the king. Most of our society today has transformed into where each one of us must work, but not all. In this book, I will explain the major changes based on my experiences as a mortgage closer or signer of legal documents as a Notary service to the public. I will also talk about the changes in our digital world. Our digital world is changing to the extreme every year. We always have changes in our cell phone styles and more.

Not only cell phones but everything we need in this world, there always be a new gadget, and or updated function of all computers and gadgets. Artificial Intelligence is, or shall I say taken over humanity's skills that it could damage humans' capabilities to function. It is too fast that some people are unable to catch up. Therefore, we will talk about the meaning of the feudalistic system. Is a Feudal System a combination of legal, economic, military, cultural, and political customs? This practice was popular in the 9th and 15th centuries of medieval Europe.

As the writer of this particular book, I am very curious about where we came from and where and how our rules regulations, and policies had been developed. Aren't we just recycling and repeating our developed knowledge of what we learned from previous eras? Such as those eras where feudalism was a practice on how the people lived and how their lives were in those times where the practices of Feudalism existed. In today's governmental and technological advances, we call it the Information Surge. The question would be if we are still in the King's compound, relying on the king to provide necessities. It is hidden, but it is in many different forms.

As we remember, a long time ago, people lived in the king's compound. The king provided food and shelter for the people but no "salary" for the people who worked for the king. Today, people work but must work eight hours a day or more and must pay sales tax, property tax, and file income tax returns. Let us define what people are paying these days, how, why, and what causes them to go this far in consumerism behavior to boost the economy. It seems like we are still living in the compound of the king, but we must work hard to earn income, and you are paying the King instead now, not anymore that the King feeds and provides shelter for you. It is you who is paying the King, and the king pays the new entrants' people in this country, the land of the free. What can we do as we, the people supposedly having freedom, we call it in this new trend of the Feudalistic Era in the 21st Century?

Chapter 1

Feudalistic Twist: Hard Workers Versus Being Disabled

In this country, the USA, the land of the free, a relief you may think that you will be saved, but again, you will be back to the ruins you were just in. Does that sound familiar? However, the system will not quit on you until you are exhausted and beat up. Then, you are done. Well, there will be some offers such as government programs and non-profit organizations to provide you with food stamps, free meals at the church, welfare, HUD, and many others.

However, this type of system I am talking about is now trying to analyze and realize but it will take time for all people to realign their lives once got ruined by this system. People learned to just play with the system for better or for worse. Of course, people select for the better. Again, you are playing with the system, and you take advantage of it so you can take all that you've lost. No. It will train you to become hooked up to something different but not cure the issues you were facing at that moment of your life. You may ask what am I talking about?

Are we trying to consider these people wrong? Now, it becomes another part of the system that you will be and become disabled and worthless to please the system. You are now getting into the life of Dependence. Dependence on the system, that is. That means you will lose your ability to work, or you intend to lose your ability to work and become dependent on the system and file disability money because you are now disabled. That's what freedom will cost you. Besides, the word freedom is misunderstood. I also mentioned the word "freedom" in my other book, the very misunderstood word, FREEDOM.

You like the name Disability because you can take and get what you want and live with the money given through the system from the people who work so hard and pay income taxes. That's where your given money came from. I know it is hidden; you can't see it because it is through the system, the Disability System Program. You are proud to be disabled.

Aren't you? It seems you are going back to living in the compound of the king but without physical labor, instead receiving disability only to ruin your capabilities to exist. Do you know how many disabled people are in this country? There are many disabled people. They are back in the compound of the king. However, double the time they received money and well taking of free food and money without working. Again, the money game is on in this issue, the Disability Status issue.

Although you lose all the benefits as humans, such as ableness, motivation, positivity, creativity, productivity,and activity, once you become part of the Dependence System group, you will lose those God-given talents. It will be taken away from you. You can't exercise the God-given talents and capabilities within you because you are now disabled and receiving money from the system, which I called in this book the Feudalistic Twist. Then, you will continue your dependency on the system as a slave, which I call the Feudalistic Era of the 21st Century.

In the beginning of Feudalism, the people relied on the King to provide everything, but you must work for the King with no compensation. In 21st-century feudalistic style, you will go through the Systems, and from there, everything is taken away from you then you will become dependent and disabled. Therefore, you now rely on the system instead of coming out of the system. There are many people involved with these types of Systems, the Disability System in this Feudalistic Era of the 21st century.

The disability system has been going on, but it was taboo; however, just lately, this type of system has been recognized and fully taken advantage of and become more visible to the naked eye. Meaning it is now becoming legalized to become disabled to be provided with money without working. The taxpayers, such as those who still work and earn income, and the hard workers are the ones paying these disabled people through filing taxes by hard workers. Partly, society is divided into two: the hard workers who refuse to be on disability and the disabled or intent to be disabled. So, the people who still work and believe in working to earn income are the ones who are paying these disabled people or intend to be disabled to get social security money for their disability, which is a hidden agenda we call Social Security Disability.

We are the cash cow for businesses, politicians, and government. Think. Through donations, co-pays, insurance, taxes, and others we pay them in an obscure way. In the era of feudalism, a decade ago, the king provided shelter and food for the community, but the family had to work without compensation. Today, we work with compensation, but you also pay sales tax, insurance, and income tax at the end of each year and many more as a collection of your living in your own country such as the king's compound.

You don't pay double what in the era of first Feudalism, where people lived with the kings and queens' compound. Today, it still exists, but it triples the way you pay the King or, shall I say, the governmental system. However, you may ask where this money was spent. Well, we can count on all of them, such as the money going to road repair and infrastructure to commute for all people who need roads to commute to work and disabled people, of course, we may say. In the 21st Feudalistic era, we must pay the

King or Uncle Sam, and we call the king these days the system. We called these monies collections, income tax, sales tax, gas tax, tax, tax, and more tax.

It is now visible, but in 1980, when it was not allowed to insert the amortization document and closing fees, it was hidden. Today, you see them all, and it is your privilege to see them and calculate them. But again, who wants to read it? If you get the money, and they get their share, document shovels under the table. Due to your busyness in life, these documents will never be seen until you suddenly need money again and again. It sounds like the system has its own legal corruption activity, it is the predatory lending and usury law.

The mortgage company can charge a fee or interest rate whatever they want for their own manipulation of the system that is hidden under those too many documents to read. In addition, with such an example as the Disability System, people would take advantage of it. That's why there were many against the new arrangement of the government system today, and such phrases say "Drain the Swamp" perhaps is part of that investigation process of corruption, and its manipulation and taking advantage of vulnerable and financially unknowledgeable society.

Another issue of our society is the "Fund Me" system that allows whoever is trying to get help through the public. It became a legalized system to ask for donations to whoever wanted to ask for money through the "Fund Me" system. Is this a "Legalized Beggar" that is asking for funds through the public? It used to be that this was illegal for the purpose of protecting the public, but not anymore these days.

It used to be that Nonprofit Organizations such as 501 C3 and other coded Nonprofit Organizations were the only ones able to collect donations from the public. A nonprofit organization is an organization that has the license to conduct its business to help the needy. Again, we may ask the question also if these types of organizations are really collecting funds or if fundraising events are truly for the needy in the community. Too many blurry activities of many organizations and individuals. It seems there are no rules and regulations, and it is just very wild out there that affects the rest of society.

Furthermore, the basic knowledge of buying and maintaining a home is now gone. We are into too many economic procedures, such as insurance, maintenance, tools, and materials that are made of plastics instead of real wood. Woods are thrown out and replaced by plastics, and now we have garbage and clogging problems all over. We wonder why there are so many homeless in an abundant country. We have become the victims, especially the homeless and the poor, due to too many fees, rules, and regulations, and real and helpful regulations are abandoned.

Companies must earn big bucks as their priority to survive in the economy, and the rest of the company will go down the drain, closed, that is. Also, some businesses are unable to survive in this type of economy that AI manages. However, there could be a new business structure by AI, such as the digital world of business. Are humans able to adapt this type of customer service from AI? In addition, people are prevented from being educated and knowledgeable, to being ignorant is where the money can be found, such as advertising promoting fear, worry, and false knowledge.

Real estate priorities are to earn big bucks, shoot for the star, and therefore have prospective and non prospective home buyers or the public in general hungry for knowledge on how to budget, and maintain an abode. We are avoiding the public to learn the basic knowledge of budgeting and maintaining a home. We are making homebuyers unknowledgeable, so a mishap and mistake will cost them, which benefits the insurance, and many other organizations cuddle them for money to get help.

A hidden secret of those many who know about it. In financial issues in this country, we, the society assumed that all, all human beings know how to budget and know how to maintain a home. Therefore, there are so many in this country, the home of plenty the and abundance are homeless and hungry. It may be that the cost of housing materials is so costly that no one can afford to buy to build a decent home.

Today's society may have to go back to the Feudalistic era, where the Kings and Queens provided food and shelter for the family. However, no monetary or salary for the workers. For me, that is a boring life that I may not have challenges on how to live and support myself with my own effort to earn income. Own income, that is. Therefore, being disabled fulfilled the ability to be under the king's rules or in today's Feudalistic in the 21st Century to be provided with two types of benefits: being disabled and having no need to work, then you will receive disability money called Social Security Disability money. Again, the money game is fulfilled for this group of disabled people. Clever!

Life then, and today has a similarity but in a twisted way. The king used to feed the family and society. However, these families must work for the king without salary. Today, we society work, and work to earn money, the hard workers that is. We use that money to support ourselves, as we call the "give me liberty or give me death" type of methodology, and we call this a free society. We are free from the hands of the king to make us what we call slavery.

Today, we are free from the compound of the king and his authority, but of course, we follow the rules and regulations intact with every decision we make. If you don't follow the rules and regulations…it is good for the company that handles this issue, so you may receive penalties for the organization to survive. Society today survives because of knowledge acquired and hard work. I do believe that we are still a slave but in a different way of handling it, and it doubles the slavery conditions than in 300 BC. (My Philosophical View See below).

My philosophical view about being a hard worker in America versus laziness relying on the government-given money for disability, disability privilege, is an overwhelming issue, and no one understands it; maybe we understand, but we just ignore it. Why? This type of issue in this country is very blurry. Blurring it to benefit the lazy people, but only to collect what is given out there. The hard-working people are the ones who were paying for this country, or shall I say, providing for the lazy people or pretending to be lazy and poor to get the benefit.

Also, really trying, I said "trying" to be poor and disabled to get the benefit. I perfectly understand that "we should help the poor and the unable," but this is not the case anymore. Lazy people and those who pretend to be poor to get benefits are very well taking advantage of the privilege of those who truly need it. If you are one of those, you probably hate this book. You may discontinue reading it.

Right?

Chapter 2
How To Get Out Of The Systems

Talk about debt free life (Rich Dad, Poor Dad book). Talk about living in an uncivilized world. The uncivilized world has the basic wisdom and knowledge that the Lord has given us. In the civilized world, the information surge contaminates the Systems, and the systems are contaminated with viruses in many forms. The uncivilized world uses Wisdom and Common Sense, not documents, rules and regulations, and many other manipulations of the human mind, such as fear.

In the Uncivilized world, there are no Systems, and they only use common sense and wisdom, but it could be that these common sense, wisdom, and consciences are seared. In the Civilized World, the Systems manipulate our actions and living style. However, we somehow use some good common sense and good conscience. Freedom is seeing the other side of the world with good common sense and good conscience, but is the other society trying to understand it or just letting it be without complaint?

In this book, let me explain to you briefly what the "money game" is. I call it within the system and within our minds as an individual to understand the system and to be manipulated by fear to purchase whatever they advertise out there in this world of confusing information surge, I called it. We will talk about mortgage loans for a moment and then move forward to insurance companies: health, home, car, and many other forms of insurance that wipe out our cash and leave nothing for ourselves.

Also, a fear tactic from commercialized credit scores so you will be able to raise or pay your owed balance. However, you didn't really owe money due to you didn't use your credit card at all! Let me tell you about my story, about my own experiences, and how I lost money without knowing about these tactics and my true ignorance of the money game ingrained in our systems. First, what is the meaning of the word "system?" The meaning of the word "system" is *"a group of interacting bodies under the influence of related forces"* or *"an assemblage of substances that is in or tends to equilibrium"* (Digital Dictionary, 2024).

The story of some other people too that I know telling me about this type of money game in the system is hidden silently, and it's a secret for most of us ignorant individuals like me. However, when we use our common sense, something is not right and seems like a fraud, but you can't put your finger on it. Only because of our consciences that went in the wrong direction of thinking and saying, "Hmmm, maybe I am wrong." However, common sense persists but you somehow ignore it.

If your real estate is in an area where there is an HOA collection every year, it is now getting too overwhelming. It is costly to keep a house or a home to live in. I will tell you about my two properties in Abbeville, Alabama. The real property I bought in the year 2004 is a walk to the big lake of Eufaula Lake, a historical lake. My property is just two pieces of land. No buildings, and no one is using them. I was paying $50 in the beginning, and now it has gone up to $300 more every year. This money from landowners or residents in the area pay this amount every year because the money is supposedly to pay for the road to keep up with all road damage and other costs such as the park maintenance facing the lake.

However, I've heard that the money was not used for that purpose. The leaders of this organization kept it in their pockets. I was very disappointed. I then attended a meeting and opened the conversation on what was going on with the road in the area. The leaders and other members were very annoyed by my questions. I was pushed out of the meeting. As I always do, if no one opens the hidden agenda, I always open it myself. Then I got in trouble. I was removed from the meeting. No one really holds me back, and the rest of the members can't say anything.

This is very sad and dishonest of and landowners in the area. You can't say anything, or you will be pushed out of the meeting, and you are not welcome at the next meeting. Exactly the same information I received from the people living there as residents of this property in Abbeville, Alabama. Therefore, I am selling my property and will never purchase another one in that area. I am selling it very cheaply, and I don't care if I lose money. I will invest my money in another area of the world instead. That's how desperate I am to get out of the system. That's just one example of the word "system."

To continue my experience of the system, one of the leaders told me to "get out." I then headed to the door, leaving the meeting. No wonder that there were only a limited number of members attending the meeting every month because they will push out if there are questions about the money, they are paying yearly in that community through Association dues. Such a corrupt organization and no one can stop these practices. We, the landowners, and the residents who owned the properties have no right to talk about it and no right to complain. If you complain, you will be pushed out the door.

Another system I would like to talk about is when you have a house, and you will apply for a mortgage loan to finance your first home and, of course,insurance for the mortgage company as first lien holder to be covered just in case there is disastrous hurricane come to the area. It's a protection for lien holder and, of course, the owner. I agree with that. The mortgage company, the lien holder, will demand the following: homeowners' insurance, flood insurance, other insurances, property tax intact, and many other requirements to protect the mortgage company just in case you, the homeowner, defaulted on your home.

Defaulted means you are unable to pay your mortgage payments and insurance, fees, fees, and more fees, etc. If this happens, you are unable to pay your mortgage payment, fees, etc., and your home goes to the mortgage company, which is the so-called first lien holder of your property. They know what they are doing, but do you know what you are doing as a homeowner?

You have a lien on your property, but you are not the only possible owner of your own property. It's the mortgage company that is the possible owner, not you. However, if you are disabled, you get lots of benefits such as lower property taxes, lower interest rates, etc., and of course, if you are a homeless person, you will get lots of benefits and a home for free sort of. So, who does not want to be disabled if you have many, many benefits as a disabled and or incapable individual? The question would be, are those individuals really disabled individuals?

An example of the property that I sold in the Panhandle Florida area, I called the Cabana, with almost three acres of land. The couple (buyers) are both disabled, and their daughter is disabled. I asked what happened why they became disabled. It is PTSD, considered as disabled; a leg can't walk considered as disabled, and the way the couple explained to me is she is very happy and proud to be disabled. The benefits this family received as disabled individuals enabled them to buy properties from that money they received.

There are many benefits to get from the system if a person is disabled, such as an informative story from the buyer of one of my properties. They were able to buy properties in the area and live a good life but still receive monthly disability money. I just do not understand the system. Here we are as hard workers working so hard to earn an income. But those who are pretending to be disabled individuals benefit from taking advantage of it because the system said so. Taking advantage of the hard workers who file income tax, pay fees, fees, and more fees, and work so hard to live. Where are our conscience and common sense in this regard?

However, there is always a consequence when an individual pretends to be a disabled and collects disability. Individuals who practice these types of disability mentality may not have peace of mind and a calm and pleasant living situation because practicing as a disabled just to get the monetary benefit may not be a suitable alibi due to common sense, wisdom, and consciences that we all have as human living here on earth of plenty interpret the process of pretending. As a passerby here on earth, living a lie is the way you live, and you can't have peace of mind and a good life of calmness and an abundance feeling of lifestyle. Honesty is the a way of living that is much better than lying about your situation to get benefits from the government will cost you in many ways. So, why pretend to be disabled?

Therefore, I can see the consequences of these ones of pretentious behaviors, and I found out that the Cabana I sold to these people was not living there because the wife was hospitalized, somehow. As I said, there will always be consequences of what kind of mentality you have, and it affects your life. Read my book titled "Two Universes of Self," and you can purchase this book at www.amazon.com and or on my website www.authordrsofiaadams.com.

Getting out of the system, some will look for opportunities out there to do something to survive. Once you get out of the system, you will feel free and freedom is within you, and you will be able to use your capabilities that the Lord has given to you since when you were born. Also, there is more to seek within you, your own capabilities, because it is within you. As being out of the Kings Compound and taken care of by the king a long time ago, humans want freedom, and here we are today. The peoples' strategies were to have their own free-spirited kind of earning income as their own efforts in it, not through by the king's command, and we call today slavery.

Today, to get out of the King's Compound, a few examples such as people selling stuff at the flea market we called it. The Flea Market is a place where merchandise is consumed and not needed in a household to be resold to earn or get a little cash to live. Freedom is an exercise called "business setting" without the hassle of rules and regulations from the government for people who are struggling to live. Unlike in the feudalistic Constantine era, the family does not need to do a Flea market because the family is supported by the King as long the man in the house is working with the King for no pay. The Obama administration did a sort of feudalistic in Constantine's era by giving welfare to most people and the ability to buy food through food stamps, HUD, and SSI (www.bing.com).

The difference, these people did not work for the King and took advantage of the privilege given.The era of Donald Trump will be different because they will release these people from the camp and let them survive out there on their own. Just like in previous eras, the people fought to get out of the King's camp and to be free, creating a partly pilgrimage surge. It does not matter what skin color and culture; most are surging to Flea Market to create income with freedom of liberty. Perhaps not all have the same causes and reasons to resale consumed products, but I would say 99% want to buy cheaper and at no cost or give away reused merchandise to live and fulfill the needs as human being living here on earth. Perhaps, in every state, human activity may differ, but the focus is to get by to live. It could be that the products they are selling are resold and resale and resold, but the results are for everyday needs and wants in life (www.bing.com).

In this Flea Market, I have been to, the people coming here to sell their resold merchandise are older citizens, and some are disabled. Perhaps to get extra cash to live and perhaps something else such as medical bills and food to eat at home. The Flea Market has existed since the feudalistic era, the time when the pilgrimage lifestyle then after the Kings Compound diminished. Such as Ireland created the first group selling artworks on the street. Today, people are selling things on the street. The cost of people's living, such as home insurance, health insurance, other types of insurance, property taxes, food, and other needs, is so costly that people are moving to other places to live cheaper lifestyles. One of my friends is already in the process of living in a tiny house so to speak on what we have these days.

Getting out of the system and using your ability and capabilities to survive gives you a free will. You will benefit from the use of your ableness, and capabilities already intact within you since when you were born. Anyway, to enforce and use your capabilities instead of not being a slave, not to take advantage of the given benefits from the system, one of many examples are the disability money and many, many more. As mentioned above, there will always be consequences when an individual pretends as disabled and collects disability money.

While continuing living, do these individuals who practice these types of disability mentality have peace of mind, calm and pleasant living? This practice loses your ability to create and earn income through persistent, hard work. I categorized these types of activities as good exercise for our well-being, creativity, and positivity for the mind and heart.

Chapter 3

Three Hundred Years (300 BC) Versus 21st Century

In those eras of 300 BC and before, humans created their own living space without Artificial Intelligence. They would eat food they planted and used, plant fruits and vegetables for medicinal purposes. Which are those plants and vegetables still exist today's world, but we somehow ignore them due to easy access to the pharmaceutical industry. Now, at the present time in the 21st century, people are developing artificial intelligence (AI), meaning it's all artificial, as what the name says.

In this 21st Century, the bad are now protected, but the good people are now abandoned. Previous centuries, when the kings versus government in the 21st century, are very similar to our leaders of today. There are many issues affecting our leaders of today. Looking back centuries ago let me briefly analyze the living situation of humanity inside the King's compound. Such example, the families were the workers for the king, and the people worked for the king for daily necessities. Today, we, the people, seek our own supplies to live but analyze it at the end of the year for income tax credit purposes instead. The inherited freedom given to all humans is constantly exercising the freedom through critically criticizing our leaders of today. In addition, leaders are constantly exercising their instinct as supposed to be leaders of the nation we are in. Perhaps going in the wrong direction, as what we have learned from the past has never been corrected through mishaps. The fight is to keep going, leaders versus people.

Therefore, we have researchers to supposedly solve the problems through case studies and research. In the research form of writing, the constructivist's (qualitative) assumption to construct knowledge is to experience and or observe individuals with those who lived with the phenomena or events. To clarify, the constructivist paradigm gathers information from a particular powerless group, the poor, which Mertens calls "unheard voices," versus the transformative paradigm gathers information from both powerless subjects (poor) and the powerful subjects (rich, politicians, etc.) sharing power together to get the best knowledge, result, and solution to a particular focus subject of study.

The article in Early Childhood Journal (2002) stated, "Fear of such harsh criticism can be surprisingly effective at keeping educators silent" (p.217). The use of the hermeneutic theory of research paradigm is complex in that it describes the participant's lived experience. The expected outcome is to understand the phenomena of "harsh criticism." What causes harsh criticism, and how to understand the result and outcome affecting children and the victims of the phenomena? How can we avoid harsh criticism without leaving the need to criticize or to judge something? The idea in the feudalism era is that the king supplies the necessities for people for everyday family needs as long you work for the king without a salary.

The family lives in the compound, such as food and shelter are supplied by the king. Today, each of us must work on our own to supply everyday needs to live. Today, we file income tax returns instead and receive earned income credits through qualifications of dependencies. Because of the population increase and the removal of the King's kingdom, we, the people, are responsible for seeking our own food and shelter, but still, the king of today, we call him Uncle Sam, remains vigilant on who gets the credits from your hard-earned income. But you may or may not get awarded if you have lots of children. Depending on what the rules and regulations are to get earned income credit called (EIC).

As a reminder, in those days, the multiplication of humanity must be exercised, but today, we may de-multiplied the production of humanity; therefore, the condom is created. Does it work? This question of mine should be answered by Human Services, which handles humanity as a group of people who serve the needs of these types of families. The new generation is producing babies in a very different manner. Today, young children are creating babies, and either neglect them, remove them from the womb, and or sell them. As we know already, these children are sold but not recognized yet, just some kind of gossip we have heard, or shall we just ignore it?

According to Dr. Shashi Punam (2020), "Human trafficking is the trade of humans, most commonly for the purpose of forced labor, sexual slavery, or commercial sexual exploitation for the trafficker or others" (Punam, page 1, 2020). This type of crime is hidden, and victims of this type of crime are reluctant to report due to perhaps the language barrier and the unknown situation, causes, and consequences of the crime, the human trafficking crime. My theory is due to the monetary needs of the individuals, the unknown consequences of their actions, and their decision that reporting this crime could hurt them. The innocents of the victims are also the causes of why this crime still exists and it's hidden.

This exploitation of humans, such as many examples of prostitution, forced labor and services, slavery, servitude, or the removal of organs to sell, profited the human traffickers. In the year 2014, just one activity of human trafficking, the profit per year, generated $150 billion (Punam 2020). Let us compare the feudalistic era in 300 BC. Is slavery still practiced today but in a different way of setting and performing? The question would be when reconnecting the past and the present, such as when the people were living in the king's compound.

Families' mainly the men in the family unit, were responsible for working for the king without pay or salary, and all life necessities were provided, such as food and shelter. Today, the slavery process is more convoluted and very confusing, and more exploitation occurs, such as selling human organs. Our system today must create a realistic and practical system that is likely to be effective in stopping these human traffickers!

Therefore, are our leaders of today effective leaders? It is us, the people of today treating our leaders like children. Such debate can up the secrecy of themselves...open it up to the whole world....it is not respect...to the leaders, but we call it the freedom of the people. There will be one day that the economy will collapse or are we here already? I understand that sometimes we do not like the leaders' policies and procedures, but their lives are exposed and made fun of without respect for our leaders, and then it could be that we are on the brink of collapsing.

Unless we find humans such as emotions, are not connected to the mind, such the Artificial Intelligence type of leaders. I do believe that respect for our leaders is needed for them to function correctly and professionally. Therefore, our leaders of today function like children, and decisions seems like it does not make sense. Examples are the squatters of today, the borders' chaos, the rules and regulations, policies, financial and health industries, school and educational systems, food and drugs, prescription drugs, and many, many more. What are squatters' rights these days?

Let me explain. In Atlanta squatters are given rights to live in abandoned or for sale homes. As the news Blaze media explains, Atlanta battles a rapidly growing squatting crisis impacting over 1200 homes. In addition, the children in school are doing essays, the formation of essays is wrong, and the teacher would appreciate the wrong writing of an essay (www.bing.com). What's going on in our society today? Something I do not understand, and maybe others do not understand either. All that was wrong, and now it is right and appreciated?

Chapter 4

Squatters' Right In Today's Economy

Squatters' rights still exist in today's generation. It was and it is. In the beginning, having property of your own, you must squat in the area where nobody owns the land. I learned this from my grandparents' story from a long, long time ago. I must research if this Squatter's Rights still exists. In today's world of rules and regulations, there are so many abandoned properties in America, the country where I was born, and perhaps other countries worldwide, too.

The tactics and strategies from the government to take care of abandoned lands and reform the lands to be marketable somehow do not make sense. However, in this new generation of the 21st Century, in some States and towns, the law even sides with the squatters, and the real owners seem to have no right to put these squatters away from the real owner's property. In Florida, however, the law is enforced to put the squatters away from the property that they occupied to respect the property owner's rights of the property (www.bing.com). It is just the right thing to do. In the King's Compound era, the society is protected by the king and nobles.

After the collapse of the Roman Empire, the feudalism era started. Society was looking for protection. Society turns to kings and nobles. "The king would grant land to nobles, the nobles would agree to fight for the king should the need arise, and the people would work the land and be under the protection of the kings and nobles" (eNotes Editorial, 23rd July 2013). However, history always repeats, and we somehow tweak it or find another way to improve. Finding ideas at different levels could also be heading toward a disastrous type of legal improvement.

Improving lands in this place means having someone live in it and creating an activity such as planting trees to revive the place. My husband and I visited the country where I was born, with 7,600 islands. This island is in the middle of every island in the area. There are more than 1,500 dialects in this country. We visited many islands to find properties for sale.

At the same time, we enjoyed the island's activities, such as island hopping, snorkeling, swimming, and many more. The people are friendly. Also, people are accommodating regarding our needs, such as looking for properties for sale, and I am so surprised because instead of being the only person to help us or to accompany us to see the property, we have 2 to 7 people assisting us in looking for property. In the USA, one person with a license shows us property, not 7 or more, to accommodate us for looking for properties for sale.

I came to find out that they do differently in this country. The people who showed us properties to sell, however, are not licensed. They get a commission from the sale of the property. I was very surprised by the no rules and regulations regarding selling properties and commission collection from the sale. There were times that I needed to ask many questions about laws and regulations, learning the way they handle real estate in the country I was born.

Also, I found out that in the area where there was no owner of the land, the barangay or the supposed leader in the area would assign a family or a person who is displaced or, shall I say, a homeless person to own the land but a condition to improve the land. Not owning though. It is assigned to take care of the land, such as being a caretaker of responsibility, planting coconuts, fruit trees, etc. However, this Assigned Owner can sell the land as long as the Assigned Caretaker/Owner has been paying Tax Declaration.

Once it is improved, the assigned owner must pay taxes, which is what they call a tax declaration. Also, once it is improved and ready to be sold, able to process title or, shall I say, ownership documentation, the Assigned Caretaker/Owner must pay capital gains. I said Assigned Caretaker/Owner because the person assigned to this abandoned, or shall I say "land no one owned it," has no documentation of a Title of Ownership. Therefore, the

Assigned Caretaker will sell the property for more because those people who showed the property will also collect a commission from the sale, and the capital gain will be shouldered by the buyer. This type of deal my husband and I did not agree with this because it seemed it didn't seem right because Capital Gains come from the gain of selling the property, which the Assigned Caretaker/Owner was given the responsibility of the property and using the property for their own need.

Therefore, philosophically, the Assigned Caretaker/Owner must pay the capital gains to BIR or DENR, not the buyer. Through the total value assessment of the property, and above the seller gains by selling this property, the seller sold, and the seller should be responsible for paying capital gains, not the buyer. However, most sellers want the buyer to pay the capital gain. It was a very confusing transaction when it came to the documentation process due to ancestry, squatter, documentation process, and ownership issues.

The documentation process takes too long, and it could take three months to more than a year to process due to those issues. In the USA title process, we called these issues NOT A CLEAR TITLE, NOT MARKETABLE we called in the USA. This means ownership right is NOT clear who owned it, and too many blockages in processing the documents for the new owner of the property because of the ancestry, unclear documentation, and the process,

In the King's Compound, in the era of the first people, there was no documentation process because, first, no one owned the property, and therefore, the king assigned the people who worked for the king. Therefore, most people living on a property were squatters, and besides no legal process, there were no rules and regulations then, and that at era was not as populated as we are today. In those eras in the 19th to 21st Century, we, the people in the entire world, are multiplying too fast. However, we are now going back to the beginning, and maybe we will be living in the King's Compound, which we call today the Government.

To continue, it was very strange to me regarding ownership of property in the country in which I was born in comparison to the USA, where I grew up from 1984 to this day. The strangest part of it is the documentation process in the country where I was born, compared to the documentation process in real estate in the USA. You buy property in the USA, and within a month, you will have your Title of Ownership recorded.

Title of Ownership should be processed as soon as possible after closing so that the new owner is entitled to the property she/he bought that day. I remember that, as a title agent since 1992 to these days as a Notary Public, the title must be processed as soon as the transaction is closed by the previous owner. For the new owner of the property bought, the owner's right is recorded, and it should be that way because it is paid, and the new owner should have the right as soon as it closed that day. The closing process and title insurance from the title company, the new documents for the new owner are legalized, stamped and recorded.

In the country where I was born, tax declaration is somehow a different process. I asked one of the sellers and those people who showed us property who have no knowledge and are not licensed to show property about tax declaration and tax Property Tax documentation. Due to the huge payment of capital gain, owners will not sell it that way to save money due to the payment of capital gain. Sellers would sell it in a monthly payment for cash buyers only for a short period of time. The first payment will be calculated as the total sale of the property.

As I used to be a Title Agent, Mortgage Closer, and a banker in America in those days when I was young, and as a Notary Public these days of retirement, I asked one of the representatives who showed us the property, but they have no knowledge at all about legality of the documentation process and no license as a real estate agent! Is this legal?

Buying property in this country is very complicated due to the documentation process. Some sellers may not be present at the table, and there are many delays, including in the survey process. This is not the only complicated process; there are many other complicated ones. There is always an "Under-the-table operation," which means giving favors to those who are processing the documents, and you give money under the table. In the USA, you can't do that. I may not buy property in this country until they are realigned by law, rules, and regulation, a thorough documentation process, and the legality of the process.

Also, foreigners cannot buy property in the country. If your wife or husband, however, was born in this country, called Balikbayan, then the wife or husband must process dual citizenship and, therefore, perhaps, awarded the right to purchase property in the area, and the inherited property from their parents, depending on the agreement between the siblings.

A foreigner buying properties in this country must go through a corporation status, and the president of the corporation must be a citizen of the country. Therefore, ownership differs, and the process can be confusing, which includes selling the property, and division can be costly. Buyers must be aware of their documentation and ownership because there are many confusing processes that could delay the documentation process and could be an illegal process of the documents. Make sure that all members of this corporation sign the papers.

Coming from the past at the king's compound to this day, we are now in the 21st century, and we think everything has changed, right? I do believe that we are just circling around a circle and repeating history, and it is still alive. However, as creative humans always have many different creativities and results, we somehow experience the best among humans in terms of creativity and productivity. Furthermore, it has reached the extreme that artificial intelligence is now being created and coming! I appreciate creativity and productivity, but not to the extreme that it loses common sense, conscience, and wisdom. I am not sure if we as humans accept this as being too extreme of creativity. What do you think?

Artificial Intelligence (AI) can kill the generation of humans' creativity and productivity. Therefore, challenges in life will be wiped out! Gone! Imagine that we, as humans, may look like zombies in the future, walking in this world without a purpose! I, myself, can't live without doing the dishwashing and cleaning the house using a vacuum cleaner. Then, here comes the AI Vacuum to clean the floor. I will become totally crazy, with nothing to do. That's just one example of how our world is changing in the other direction, which could damage humanity and its creativity and productivity.

Furthermore, in the United States of America, can these abandoned properties be bought by those investing in real estates to do a productive to revive the abandoned states. A group of firms can get together to buy abandoned lands and/or property owners who are unable to pay or take care of land and mortgages. They called themselves "Cash Buyers." But they would buy your property at a very, very low price. Their marketing strategy is as if you do not want to take care of the land anymore, or the owner is unable to pay taxes, and many more strategic wordings and selling tactics for the owner of the property to sell their lands. As I used to be a title agent, currently a mortgage closer, and Notary Public, I had never encountered such confusing documents about title processing and documentation when I was working in Hawaii, New Jersey, and Florida.

Will AI be the guide for these organizations to revive these cities? Bridgeport and Bombay, California, Fort Stevens, Oregon, Garnet, Montana, Santa Claus, Arizona, Texas and New Mexico, Wichita, Kansas, Cape Romano Florida, Fredericksburg, Virginia, Gary Indiana, Mansfield, Ohio, Staten Island and Dutchess County, New York, New Bedford, Massachusetts, and many, many more abandoned properties and businesses just to name a few (http://www.bing.com).

However, having my own property in Florida, there was a little bit of a confusing process, such as previous surveys and information about the property environment regarding weather changes, such as flooding in the area. Twenty years ago, the area we bought was not in the flood zone. So therefore, along the way, depending on how many years you have lived in the area, the area is now considered a flood zone area. The survey should have been changed to a flood zone, but this process was very slow, and selling my house now in the flood zone created an issue. The issue was that in the record, the area is a flood zone area, but in my survey, the property is not in the flood zone. The time difference and the constant ordering of surveys for new information in the area regarding the property environment also cost money.

Today, because many residents lost their primary houses in addition to many migrants that are homeless, squatters are so visible. Squatters would occupy the property if no one lived in the house. The law of trespassing has somehow been ignored. However, in Florida, squatters have no rights in properties that are either abandoned or empty. Therefore, laws and regulations are still intact in Florida State. Shall we say that in the 21st century there are so many abandoned properties?

Therefore, these properties must be sold at very, very low prices to renew and revive the area for new ones. Again, this is the beginning of recycling, repeating history, and we are here already at the King's Compound; living within these compounds, we are slaves. However, there are properties given away, but you need to work on them, and they could not be yours when it comes to the documentation process. This is similar to the era of lands given away and giving rights to squatters to stay on the property that people had abandoned.

Have you heard about these free-living spaces or free land and houses for couples that are able to produce children and have free money living in the country I am talking about? But this family could multiply as the belief before. Agreements to new residence: if the residence or husband and wife produce a family unit with children, you get support from the government or given money to the family unit. It is coming, and I wonder what's going on with humanity these days. My curiosity brought me to do research about it and find out why we humans need to multiply. It was just the previous generation. We are too many to live in his world of plenty. These are the findings about countries that needed people to live on land or houses that people abandoned or perhaps were unable to sustain the cost of having a home.

Chapter 5
The Modern Slaves

How do we consider ourselves as Modern Slaves in this generation in the 21st Century and beyond? The questions would be about how much we pay for insurance for everything we own. For example, cars, houses, floods, and more. The manipulation of scary tactics created fears in every person living with properties such as houses, investments properties, cars, boats, motorcycles, etc. The rules and regulations are a manipulation of what you have supposedly to enjoy and the hard work you've created. There are responsibilities behind it; that is what insurance companies impose on all hard workers in this world.

Are we the people, the system, and the mortgage industry's modern slaves? Do we truly live a free lifestyle, or do we, the people, must choose to live a free lifestyle? It could be that each one of us has a different meaning of a free lifestyle. Let us define it so that we can understand our positive decision to live a FREE lifestyle. However, if our lifestyle is to consume, although we do not need these kinds of stuff that are in the market, we buy them because of our mentality to consume without thinking it costs money to consume products that are not needed in our everyday living.

Consumerist behavior affects us all in many ways. Buying a means is that the behavior of unconscious buying benefits the economy and ruins people's lives for those who are out of control. Whether the product you bought benefits the buyer or not, it will ruin the buyer financially later. Those who will be affected most are those unaware of what they are buying due to compulsive behavior. The opposite effect is the economic boom, and businesses will prosper. For instance, mortgages, prescription drugs, credit cards, debit cards, technology, membership fees, insurance, donations for causes, utility bills, technology/gadgets, and psychological manipulation of the mind through fear tactics people buy, for instance, insurance policy.

Due to consumerism behavior, people suffer from those who are not aware of compulsive spending. Spreading fear is the key to economic prosperity. The population has very little knowledge of compulsive buying and is unaware of this tactic. Because their action seems to benefit them in the present time, but later, it will cost their lives. Society has no time to check information in "Fear Tactic" commercialism because of work busyness. Society trusts the system in this regard. Society does not believe that this happens here in America because we always believe that the American system is honest to people. When people work, we serve the government by paying taxes and consuming products for the sake of the economy.

Whether the product is to sell your assets such as real estate, the face-to-face tactic we hear on television has a connotation of scare tactic and manipulation of the mind you can't refuse. We, the people, are used, and or shall I say, tools for experimentation purposes of the process as being consumed and to consume. We ignore the manipulation of consumerism tactic, or shall we call it "psychologically manipulated to consume." Due to commercialization, the technique and marketing may sound right to hear.

Secondly, the fear tactic works for too many of us, especially those who are unknowledgeable in refinancing and buying real estate. We are not just talking about real estate products but any other kinds of products in the market that we, the people, consume. But again, such an example in real estate, we try to calculate it, and we know deep within our mind and heart that it seems it is not right. However, due to the desperation of needing cash to live, we are sunk into marketing tactics and the mentality of having a white picket fence and pride within in that moment of imagination.

It is right that all you gain from real estate just goes to documentary fees, title fees, realtor commissions, etc. Again, let us consider that these types of companies must also earn to survive. How about Mortgage Insurance? Who is really protected from being a homeowner by paying the mortgage insurance? Thus, what about homeowner's insurance, appliances insurance, car insurance, and many, many more insurances? Don't forget to count the premium you need to pay first before getting your money from the insurance that you are paying every month! Make sure common sense applies in this category of money game!

We will not forget that there is another way how to get money from consumers, such as selling your property, which can cost you lots of fees, as mentioned: realtor commission, documentation fee, title fee, recording fee, and more. Perhaps, on the negotiation table, costly fees can be arranged? Not really, because it is arranged by the entity. Therefore, when selling your property, be aware of what you are paying and what those fees are for. Is it worth it? Is this rule already ingrained within us, and is it difficult to trace back and question it all?

Shall we say we have learned rules and regulations tailored in the Bible and are used everywhere in the world? Perhaps you are smart enough for the money game system. That means you use my money, and I use yours, and we temporarily benefit from it? I said the word "Temporarily." the "Money Game," the cash must be circulated. However, if you do not know how to circulate, then you will lose! Although, just lately, buying a home can be shortened from 30 years to 15 years, your house just bought being mortgaged to 30 years is more profitable to the mortgage, insurance, and maintenance industries.

Writing this book, I noticed that mortgage companies are now allowing 15-year mortgages. In this country, for 30 years, the choice of the length of mortgage has always been ignored, and the 15-year mortgage has always been ignored. A fifteen-year mortgage saves the homeowner's money. With a thirty-year mortgage, a homeowner would pay interest more than a 15-year mortgage. However, homeowners must have the ability to pay higher monthly payments and, at closing, must prepare cash to pay closing costs. Previously, this benefit to homeowners was taboo until just recently, when it was offered by a few mortgage companies.

In the country where I was born, the mortgage loan can be for 2, 5, 10, and 15 years only. There is no offer for a 30-year mortgage in the country where I was born. In the era of the King's Compound, there were no problems with mortgage payments because the king paid it all!

As we all know, homelessness in California is very alarming. We may ask what happened before homelessness occurred. Besides, the fire destroyed homes in California, and drugs and homelessness are warning signs of the State of California heading to poverty issues and humanity problems. And there are more states that are heading or maybe already there to poverty. Are we just pretending nothing happened? Shall we compare this country, the USA with the third-world countries?

Bank fees, closing costs, and many other fees in buying a home can be scary to most.

The technique for some real estate buyers is to do an Owner Financed Mortgage that can be done in the Title Company with a minimal fee.

Many questions about what is going on with the conventional type of mortgage system. It does not make sense anymore to have a house to live in, they say. Some would rather rent than buy a house with a white picket fence. Then some would say to be smart in living in a tiny house, RV, van, old school bus, campsite, or any type of vehicle able to set a place to sleep, which today is now the trendy style of most used to-be home buyers.

However, be watchful because psychological manipulation will come to tiny house buyers. It could sound like you are buying a big house instead of a tiny house, and it is coming. Therefore, my husband and I are preparing for that type of lifestyle, with no mortgage and to live on a cash basis only. Therefore, we are in the process of testing the water outside the United States of America, the land of the free, abundant, and plenty. Is it really?

Land ownership in the country where I was born is very confusing in terms of legality and documentation. While my husband and I were looking around for land or a house on the beach, it was so surprising. We have encountered some difficulties understanding the documentation process, such as Tax Declarations, Not titled property, inability to have Title for Ownership, Deed of Sale, timberland type of property, agrarian, foreigners unable to purchase property, and more. There is no title company to process documentation, and only those who you know but are not licensed individuals to process documents.

In America, the land of the free, I am currently a Notary Public working with many mortgage companies and title companies. I was also a title agent from 1992 to 2004. Previously, from 1989 to 1993, I was in the banking industry, working full and part-time in 1992 in Hawaii and in New Jersey. So, when searching for property for sale in the country where I was born, I was very confused about the documentation process, such as clear titling and the tax declaration process.

In comparison to America, the documentation process is simple and clear; for example, when you buy it, you have your title of ownership, period. In America, the Title Company will be the one to process all documentation and ensure that you, the buyer, and the new owner get a clean and clear title of the property. Title agents are licensed individuals. Title agents must go through a process of being certified, learning about titles and land ownership, land selections, and the process of documents. The goal of buying a property is to have a CLEAR TITLE, which is the focus on having a property processed by the title company.

You have title insurance, which means you are insured to have a clear title of ownership of the property you bought. Buyers are protected when buying real estate in the United States of America. Is there any documentation process that does not make sense? As a title agent and a closer and signer of a mortgage here on American soil, I know the process is all DOCUMENTED. The mortgage company, as a first lien holder, will make sure that documents are processed correctly.

That's the positive side of it. Well, because the mortgage company is the FIRST LIEN HOLDER of the house you just bought, and you got the money from the mortgage company. However, if you are buying property on a cash basis, that's what I meant: no mortgage company to make sure that your documentation process is in the right condition or, shall I say, the right direction. Are you protected from being a cash buyer of real estate?

In this case, the Title Company should make sure that you have documentation in the right direction to protect you as a buyer and that documentation is correctly processed. In America, a Title Company is always there just in case you are to buy cash or real estate on American soil only. In the country in which I was born, there is no Title Company to process your documents correctly. You can hire an attorney, but it will cost you more than having Title Company process your real estate documents.

The person to process is NOT licensed, and the realtors are referral salespersons only and are NOT licensed realtors. Well, in the next book, titled The Money Game, I will explain the countries I researched about the process of buying real estate. To me, it's just very confusing, but we will see what's going on in the real estate industry in other countries based on my experiences and others I've encountered.

In the feudalistic era of 300 Before Christ (BC) and After Christ (AC), your living space was owned by the king, and you were provided with food and shelter. However, you didn't have a salary while working for the king. In this era of feudalistic society in the twenty-first century, I called it, it is your responsibility to provide yourself and your family with food and shelter, plus you are also paying the king, which we call today Uncle Sam or the Government. As mentioned above, through property tax, sales tax, income tax, and many more taxes to pay to Uncle Sam. My question would be, which one do you choose? Do you want to live with the king in the compound, or outside the compound of the king?

Let me answer those questions for you. There are so many homeless these days in America and everywhere in this world of plenty due to many, many manipulations of rules and regulations for the leaders to partly take their share, and such disastrous weather intently ruins the homes of the living. Is the disastrous weather a manipulation to create a living such as a collection of flood insurance, fire insurance, and many more types of insurance? I will leave this question for you as a reader of my book. Check it out and maybe do some research and try to understand these things, which, to me, do not make sense. Go ahead, let me know and send me your response and comments through this book, or send me your comments through my email laurdendavis@gmail.com

However, let us talk about the merging of companies these days. Their mission and vision statements may be similar, but they are different forms of understanding. As such, my husband and I travel internationally and use our so-called privileges, such as the Wyndam Card, to count our points once we use Wyndam Hotels for our stay while traveling. We stayed at one of Wyndam's hotels, which is called Wyndham Hotel, on the wall sign and on top of the roof. We signed in to find out this hotel was not Wyndham Hotel regarding their policies and procedures, such as points to be taken out from the bill for the room we used. That is just one of the examples of a very confusing type of business these days and non-coordination between merging companies.

I have noticed employment issues these days. Somehow, there are no applicants applying for jobs available anywhere anymore. I wonder why. Well, this is what I found. First, I will briefly state the disability of the workers. Today, it's better to be disabled than a worker. Disability earns more, and workers do not. So, it is no wonder there are no more workers applying for jobs but showing themselves as disabled. How do I know this type of silent activity of humanity? My tenants, buyers of the property I sold, and many other conversations I have with our neighbors and those disabled people's stories. What happened to the government rules and regulations?

Well, to make the story short, people are revolting and want to take advantage of the privilege of most disabled individuals and the illegal merging in the United States of America. Also, the disabled, are they really disabled? Well, pretending to be disabled is living a good life, they say, then those working so hard and paying so many taxes and high cost of insurance are so behind in life. So, as you can see, there are many disabled people applying for disability money. There are many companies looking for people to work, but nobody is applying anymore.

Chapter 6

Our Leaders Now & Then

Previous leaders like the Kings and Nobles were the ones who managed the people, and previous societies had no freedom of their own. In the 21st century and in previous generations, leaders need followers; therefore, they will go to lengths to search for who is to be the follower. In the previous leadership style, if the people did not follow the command from the king, their families would be starving, or they would get killed if they didn't follow the King's demands and authorities. Whether the goals are for another group of people or not or for our children for the next generation, today's leader's goals do not matter at all. Overall, those who have a leadership role must have confidence in what they say and what they decide.

Supposedly, that's what a leader is all about in this century and previously. Leaders look to their subordinates to make sure that they are comforted, assisted, and serviced. Leaders must serve their subordinates. Genuine leadership is of only one type: supportive. It leads people: It doesn't drive them. It involves them: It does not coerce them. It never loses sight of the most important principle governing any project involving human beings, namely that people are more important than things. Leadership is not an ego game. Leadership means responsibility. Leadership means setting aside personal desires. Leadership means service. Leadership means loyalty. Leadership is intuition guided by common sense. Are our leaders of today doing what they are supposed to do for ALL people, not just their followers?

Let us talk about what true success in leadership is. A true leader is neither attached to success nor afraid of failure. A project can be destroyed, but never energy itself. How can you be a leader in an area where there are no followers? For example, an advocate for the public may not be enough to persuade them to join the organization. A few reasons why: 1) It could be that speech selected by a few people may be misunderstood. Secondly, cultural ideology and belief could be the reason. Every culture always has a different belief for each one of us.

Here in the United States of America, we are allowed to agree and disagree, but there are times when consequences occur due to disagreement and agreement conversation or belief of each culture. In business, if you are a new entrant in a community where 99% of people are in one culture, and you are another type of culture opening a business, then there will be what we call the new entrant, an invader, so to speak. Who am I to tell them what they think about? Therefore, we always rely on education about many diverse cultures. That is the question most of us would ask. But deeper inside our minds and hearts, there is confusion about who we are as a society. We somehow isolate ourselves to say that we are not like that, and we pretend that we are on the other side or the other way around.

According to Singh B.R. in Abstract (ISSN:1467-5986), "Granting this, teachers and educators should be asking themselves: what positive conditions, norms and principles make dialogue across cultures possible and what can they do to promote those conditions norms, some guidelines for the conduct of dialogue across cultures. By being conscious of the successes and failures, as well as aims and objectives, one can be clearer about how to proceed. It could be in discussion or conversation with an individual across many diverse types of cultures here in America on what to expect (Abstract Page ISSN:1467-5986).

Therefore, education is very important these days. However, do our teachers teach and act as teachers in the classroom? Everything is changing in this era of education because some teachers also are not good examples for their students. Common sense and good conscience are not used anymore by these so-called Professionals.

Good ethics and good morals are now thrown into the pit of the devil's way that turns into unethical and immoral activities of humanity. Our children are also affected very much by how they grow up in an immoral society, and therefore, we hope our children learn and gear their attention to seek the right way of living. However, even the traditional words we have been using is now changing. Check your dictionary such example: the word "immoral vs amoral."

Today, we always hear the bad and the immorality of our society today, and we silence the good, right, and good morals in life that we are supposed to carry on, spread the good news for us to ingrain the right way of living. Our leaders of today supposedly guide the young and the old through the right direction, but the way they carry themselves is like children of the dump. Our children's brains are still in the process of growing, and therefore, we somehow ingrained our children into the immorality of these generations.

Before Covid 19, I was a business owner and a consultant in the art, and I was invited to be a vice president of an organization. I made an excuse not to be part of it because I was not able to take responsibility but because being a leader is not a respectable position to be in anymore. People have no respect for their leaders anymore.

It is a scary position to be in. This is the same feeling I have when it comes to a higher position in the company. I'd rather be to have my own organization to truly serve the people. I do serve not because of people's demands, which some or most leaders serve, but because of the people they serve for their own good. Perhaps we may question today that our leaders are backing out from leadership responsibility.

I did not take any political curricula in my college and scholar days, but only Leadership in Public Service, which is my specialty. As an observer from outside the box, I see the political setting as entertainment in a comedy arena, and performers such as politicians become clowns for the crowd to laugh at.

At the time, as a PhD candidate in public service leadership in human services specializing in nonprofit management and leadership, I realized that these actions are truly recipes for scrutiny. Therefore, our leaders of today are not in tune with what society is screaming about. Leaders of today are there on the podium to be laughed at and to develop their own agenda and entertainment for publicity. Their goal of solving problems such as economic crises and health care is not effective.

Leaders lose followers, and followers gear their attention toward self-rule. Previously, as a consultant of a newly formed organization where I mentored two candidates, I could feel and see the struggle of Green horn leaders. New leaders always think about their feelings as our politicians today think of themselves as children and new unskillful leaders of the U.S., which is laughable. No wonder society is criticizing the leaders of today.

Similarly, the new development leaders that I mentor are at least not laughable because these leaders are new and only lead a few followers, volunteers, and employees. Unlike the presidential candidates and other politicians in their own leadership roles who supposedly lead the United States of America, America is a nation with a diverse population from different countries. America is not just America but represents the whole world. Therefore, the behaviors and practices of our leaders affect us all, society, and one of many examples is the criticism of our leaders today.

Are the assumptions of "harsh criticism" received by leaders, such as volunteer leaders, board members, community leaders, and schoolteachers prominent today? Are there connections between independent variables (harsh criticism) and dependent variables (leaders) affecting our children's ability to choose a career after high school due to bad leadership of our higher ranking in society? Is there significance to the problem, such as those influential figures to our children of today being harshly scrutinized? To specify one of many cases, there are performances that are harshly criticized, such as the early childhood educators' affecting their ability to teach our young minds of today.

When high school children choose a career or continue their education to a higher level, they somehow choose a below level non-leadership role for a career or education. The theory was that a higher level of education expects a higher level of responsibility. Therefore, there are many children who have less than high school graduates or are educated and graduated only in high school, with no motivation to move forward due to low choices of education knowledge; they think it is a better choice. Why?

The research I did was to examine the relationship between harshly criticized educators and our young school children. Secondly, the objective of the study was based on finding the "known" and "the unknown" phenomena of "harsh criticism." Harsh criticism is a trend in organizational settings, politics, and the community that affects the children of today. Saiya's (2009) article expresses concerns about who's raising our children of today. She continued that educators and schools are not the right community to raise children, but parents are.

However, educators and schools are to be blamed by parents concerning these issues. Her article titled: "Who's Raising Our Children" has a connotation that television, radio stations, the internet, and games are raising our children of today. Parents should have control of their children. However, since most parents are at work every day, children are forced to entertain themselves through television, video games, and the internet. How do these phenomena affect our children of today?

The interviews with organizational leaders, political leaders, and community leaders were explored and examined (Davis, 2014). So, what is really a leader's responsibility? Develop laws and regulations and protect society from any harm it may encounter. Therefore, laws and regulations must be implemented. However, always carry on the basic and necessary common sense, wisdom, and conscience in the process.

Because there are sometimes very confusing activities in the society that are hard to differentiate and understand, common sense must be applied. For example if people were allowed to get into the United States without paperwork, what would happen in the cities of the USA? People who come to the USA through the borders must be documented before being accepted into the country of the United States of America.

However, in our society today, consumerism behavior creates issues and also ruins particular individuals in that regard. Common sense and good conscience do not apply due to confusion between good and bad common sense and conscience. Confusion begins with these societies we are building here in the USA and perhaps all over the world. Let us see what's going on.

Chapter 7

The New Frontier: Consumerism Behavior Of Today

Technology today is changing from Facebook to the internet, artificial intelligence, email, paying your bills, from television, to watching movies these days, and your billing arrangements are now through online. What's next? Transhumanism which my husband and I talked about after dinner is a transformation of "the belief or theory that the human race can evolve beyond its current physical and mental limitations, especially by means of science and technology." Is transhumanism a movement, the enhancement of human condition to be widely available? (Google, 2024).

We, as humans may lost our capabilities, the natural ways of capabilities such the Almighty has given to all of us, the humans, such one of the many examples that has been already exercised by humans is the misunderstanding the meaning of morality versus immorality. Good common sense, consciences, and wisdom will no longer be used in the future, and is it already here? As of today, merging issues of these immorality is already existed and visible. Transhumanism symbols are the transcending the limitations of the human body and mind, to add and go beyond.

Are we already in this type of transhumanism phenomenon? How close are we to the type of transformation of humanity? Well, it's already here or perhaps soon there will be an advanced transformation of humanity, perhaps in the year 2030 (Google, 2024).

Let me ask you how costly it is to those who are intently misinformed and being misled by advertisements, and propaganda these days. Is this event and changing has something to do with merging by companies? Misinformed of no fault can be costly for us consumers. Misinformation of the merged company we may say that it is not the fault of the other system as we use an excuse can be costly to consumers.

Such information on electronics, banking, writing, news, mortgages, investments, and many, many more industries are changing course in serving the consumers. What is happening to our laws and regulations these days in protecting consumers? Shall we as consumers situate ourselves in finding out first before making decision on what company we must use in regard to mortgage, insurances, financial, and or buying products to make sure it is legit, or real? Where is Consumer Protection these days?

For a few examples here, regarding getting a loan for buying investment property misinformation of appraisal charges, and building inspection fees, etc. Misleading information in VA

Loans for 100 % taken from equity of your home. What's the difference between a 30 year and 15-year loan. Now some mortgage company is talking about a 15-year loan because people are acknowledging the cost of having a 30-year loan.

However, the previous mortgage industry is enjoying the big gain for 30-year loan. Mortgage in the country I was born is not offering a 30-year loan mortgage because it will cost the consumer money to take a 30-year loan. In comparison, here in America we think the mortgage companies are now becoming like a 3rd world mentality. I can sense it that the new world is becoming the 3rd world, catching up with the losses and or maybe trying to gain more due to the naivety of the consumers. Taking advantage of consumers being misinformed. Again, we may say depending on what the consumer needs. But really, you, as a person who develops an organization, a company for consumers and gearing towards misinformation and misleading unknowledgeable people regarding mortgages and your policies, for me, is an unethical act of those companies and organizations.

How about social media, messenger, carrier, and job information? Being knowledgeable of little pieces here and there through social media, we may say let us put the pieces together, may not be enough. The knowledge we know through social media can be convoluted information. Because of our very busy lifestyle, being misinformed can be add to the disaster of seeking the right information for our needs these days. In this information age, instead of seeking to be knowledgeable, we may cut down on the clutters of knowledge and downsize the information we have received. Sometimes, it does not make sense when you put together the information we have received. One of the simple examples,

How did we humans exist in this world? Let me explain first how the earth circulates for the plants and animals to survive. My book titled "Two Universes of Self" explains the earth and the human body. The Bible also states that struggles in life make us stronger, and challenges give us more strength to survive in our surroundings, earth, the land of plenty. Humans do the same. Humans are creative and talented, and with many talents, some use them to take advantage for a purpose, and or bad and good.

I do believe that humans use this manipulation of privilege. It is, perhaps, the challenges they go to that their minds can create, and of human's power within, we call Spirituality and the Worldly existence within human's thought Universe. Let me explain briefly: Spirituality, such as the Holy Spirit and Soul within us, the unseen elements with every human on earth that includes all living things such as animals, insects, and plants. However, with these huge changes within us, Artificial Intelligence seems to be taking over our thought processes. Have you noticed that it is very important to know about our humanity these days?

We need to wake up! It is crawling to every technology we have and connected within our minds. In addition, let us define the structure of our family unit system. It is used to be that women were kept by men and once a woman marries a man, therefore, a man is responsible of the woman's needs, food and clothing then they have children.

Children are taken care of by the wife. She is responsible for taking care of children, cleaning, and cooking. The man or husband looks for money. He works to bring the money in the house to support the family. Today, it is now reverse. But of course, it is still in the mind of others the previously learned behavior of humanity. How about in the now era of Artificial Intelligence? The world is changing fast!

In our current situation so far, the wife brings the money, and the husband stays home to take care of children, clean and cook. There are men doing that but not all yet. I have encountered men work so hard to earn money and at the same time taken care of their children because their wives are busy drinking alcohol and having an affair with many different men. However, again, Artificial Intelligence will change it all! It is coming! In our society no one notices these types of events because we are focus and engrained that women were the victims by men. Few examples of case studies of humans here on earth, their choices created havoc in their own lives.

A man looking for another woman for the reason of missing character of the first wife, for that reason alone, there will be another reason why divorce is very prominent these days. The disunite of family unit is the very many practices of men and women to these days, and the previous and this generation. Because of the result of the previous generation's family disunity, this generation may not be interested in getting married. Therefore, intimate relationship activity for this generation is just to have intimacy activity for a temporary intimate relationship that ruins their lives.

+ **Case Study #1:** John's Story is about getting married and then remarrying to find a woman who would fill in the missing character of the first wife. However, going through this type of pattern only creates more havoc because he ends up taking care of children and paying child support from first to second to third wives. This type of decision making should already be thought about before acting and making it into reality. Therefore, John works so hard to support 6 children from 3 different wives. We didn't even mention the financial struggle that also suffers when there is disunity in the family unit.

+ **Case Study #2:** Tim's Story- Tim has had one wife since he got married. However, adopting many children for the wife to be happy with the caring side of a woman was probably too much to handle due to responsibilities such as money and business. Therefore, his wife's attention was always on the children who were adopted. The longing for having many children removed that ability to relate to your partner in life because there are responsibilities to be fulfilled in every child you adopted. Communication, and unity with your wife or husband will be diminished. That's why a man or a woman, or a husband and or a wife will find another connectivity between a feeling of as a husband and wife. Therefore, family unity will collapse. Of course, that includes income, or shall I say, financial stability for the family unit also will be disrupted.

✦ **Case Study #3:** The story of Thomas is very chaotic and finally at the end he found some peace of mind that it continues his life to the end living here as a temporary here on earth of plenty and abundance. It begins when he is at his age 20s, and got married with a woman, and with the first-born son. However, his wife was promiscuity. His wife was having an affair with other men, I said men because it is more than one. While Thomas at work to earn income, his wife was busy with other men. He was wondering whether the first son was his son. This type of thought created a vine connecting the past and the present while the first was born and died in his 50s.

Most of the family unit case studies must earn income to survive to live a decent life with a white picket fence type of living. We must earn income, unlike in those eras where people in the king's compound are all provided with food, shelter, and daily necessities. Today, we are the ones who provided the king through income tax at every year process, and of course every time we buy something, we must pay sales tax, tax, and more tax. There are many more stories on how families can disunite and ruin the family unit.

Dave Ramsey, the author of "The Money Answer Book" will be one of many books to read for us to be able to start on how to get out of the system we are in. He said, "Top two ways to be smart are: 1) Say "no" to credit cards, 2) Make a budget, write it down, give a dollar a name (Ramsey, pg. 1). However, being in the system already I was thinking of living in the place where there is no system of money of some kind.

It would be very difficult for anyone to get out of the system because we are already embedded in it like a coated lollipop candy. Dipper down to the end of the lollipop stick, you will taste the bitterness of life due to System. Some people get off the system to take advantage of welfare money and other hidden benefits such as food stamps, government help, and many others.

Some will just let it collapse their lives, such as bankruptcy, litigation, and making themselves disabled to collect disability, to name a few.

Some information from people I talked to commented that being disabled in this country is for those people who "do not want to be a slave." I somewhat agree and disagree. Why do I agree? The disabled people are given money, but they cannot work and make themselves to be disabled to get benefit from the government as disabled. When they work it is always under the table. Today, we are in a different walk of life with artificial intelligence now part of our lives these days. The way earning income these days is now from home, and perhaps AI is part of that type of work environment changes.

For example, self-driving cars, banking systems such as banking online, educational system such as taking classes online, dictionary words are changing, slang and jargons are acceptable specially on Facebook, and other information communication through FB and messengers. Are we concerned about spelling and correct words to use? Again, AI is programmed by an individual or the creator of Artificial Intelligence. Hinton's work *"has potentially hastened the future he fears, in which AI becomes superhuman with disastrous results"* (Hinton, 2023 page 25).

Chapter 8

Humans Vs. Pro-Humans (AI)

Artificial Intelligence is ARTIFICIAL, which means, not real in comparison to HUMAN is real, such as humans having consciences, wisdom, and common sense. These common senses, consciences and wisdom, the spiritual world come from neurons, veins, and the flesh body of a human being. An ongoing AI is made of manipulation of images, words, sounds, and language beyond human capabilities. Artificial Intelligence is all about intelligence in an artificial way (AI), from information surge in the banking industry, health, and many more industries stealing the capability from humans to create their own ideas and abilities. Artificial Intelligence will wipe out humans on earth.

However, AI has no truth about being humans. Humans have feelings, and AI is made up by humans and it is artificial. Bannon and Allen said in the War Room "Artificial Intelligence" is the Devil here on earth (War Room, 2024). Also, they talked about that the makers of AI are smarter able to create Super Artificial Intelligence. This AI creator created an AI a machine would be killing people in way taking out the capability of humans in a natural way, and group it together to imitate human's capability. Is AI anti-Christ? (Bannon & Allen, War Room part 2).

According to Yuval, "AI has just hacked the operating system of human civilization. The operating system of every human culture in history has always been language. In the beginning, was the word we used language to create mythology and laws to create gods and money to create art and science to create friendships and nations. For example, human rights are not a biological reality. They are not inscribed in our DNA" (Harari, 2020). As humans we are the ones who created languages, storytelling, writing, and another knowledge we have within us guided by our consciences, common senses, and wisdoms the unseen world of spirituality such as soul and holy spirit.

However, in this age of Artificial Intelligence, human's creation of AI, does it all. Humans will lose the capability of what we as humans supposedly in spirituality within every human must do and create. We will become paralyzed human beings soon, and it's coming! How about schooling or shall I say, higher education for humans? Universities and schools will be gone too! AI handles everything humans want to know and learn. Jobs will be gone, and humans will be wiped out on earth. How about judges, medical doctors, and PhDs? Is AI handling the courtroom?

I am a writer to this generation, and soon, I may not be the one to write my books anymore. It could be that AI will be the one to give me ideas, tools, knowledge, and many more, but our brains and capabilities will be neglected. Therefore, humans, the real humans, will be diminished. We, as humans, are not usable anymore, then we all will die, and Pro-humans will exist. That is my prediction. Another example is Harari's article, which says that banking systems such as banknotes are now worthless. Our documentation process will now be paperless. It is now, 90 percent of the money in the world is in the form of electronic storage. In addition, stories, images, electronics, politics, children's essays in schools, laws and regulations, rules, biblical changes of holy scriptures, and fake news are already in the arena.

Are we going to believe everything we hear and see now that reality is being manipulated by AI? Just remember that every human has different ideas, knowledge, and likes and dislikes. How can AI be developed by humans to create and re-group every human's mentality? How? In addition, in the religion arena, it is now changing. Such examples given by Harari, "Q Anon cult has formed around anonymous online texts known as queue drops now followers of this cult which are millions now in the US and the rest of the world collected reviewed and interpreted these Q drops as some kind of new scriptures" (Harari, 2024).

The big question would be is an AI able to insert emotions from humans to the disk of an AI? According to Harari, 2020 *"Non-human alien intelligence which knows how to exploit with superhuman efficiency the weaknesses biases and addictions of the human mind and also knows how to form deep and even intimate relationships with human beings that's the big question already today in games like chess no human can hope to beat a computer what if the same thing happens in politics, economics and even in religion when people think about changing PC and the other new AI tools" ((Harari, 2020)).*

Artificial intelligence (AI) does not need feelings and emotions. AI unable to learn real consciousness, common sense, and wisdom as all humans have. Unless, humans have seared consciences, and common senses. Does AI able to create seared consciences and common sense too? How? Therefore, if AI has intimacy feeling developed it must be that it is fake, and it's programmed by the maker of AI, the humans. God created humans, and I do believe.

How can AI be a human when human created AI? Artificial Intelligence (AI) cannot develop conscience, common sense, and wisdom that all humans have it. But in the level of well functioned, for example, good conscience, common sense, and wisdom, not the seared and disturbed. Choices in life are too overwhelming due to Information Surge through AI made by humans, not God who made living things here on earth of plenty.

I always put in my writing, common sense, consciences, and wisdom are our tools to be humans, not pro-humans or shall I say Artificial Intelligence (AI). However, the creator of AI is now planning to insert emotions like humans within the artificial intelligence pro-humans within. What should we do in the next generation if this gets worse, or is it? You can send your comments on my email laurdendavis@gmail.com and let me know your opinion and suggestions.

According to The Economist The World Ahead 2024 magazine stated that "Companies across industries are using AI to supercharge growth and build engines of innovation" (Economist, 2024). My theory is that AI helps companies to navigate a future which is uncertain at this moment. Such that in the future but it is unlimited to a point that AI will take of every need in the company such as real ideas, value, and supposedly deliver results of the companies' need. Therefore, involvement with Artificial Intelligence processes will continue in the near future. Let us give a few examples here such as banking in digital world, are they going to survive?

Replacing the ability of humans to do to make it easier for humans such thinking using the brain to think of humans is very important to function the brain cells. This activity will be taken away and will be replaced by AI. Is AI having a genome, and or chromosomes, veins, blood, and many other real body elements of a human? *"Alarmed, Hinton left his post as VP and engineering fellow in May 2023 and gave a flurry of interviews in which he explained that he had left in order to be able to speak freely on the dangers of AI—and his regrets over helping bring that technology into existence. He worries about what could happen once AI systems are scaled up to the size of human brains—and the prospect of humanity being wiped out by the technology he helped create"* (Hinton, 2023 page 24).

Now writing this book of mine that according to Time Magazine (Marsa, 2023 page 23) the AI jobs available right now for AI to function are: the Engineering such as research scientists, Machine learning, data engineering, robotic, data scientist engineering, business consulting, Sales positioning, and ethicists engineering (Time Magazine, page 37). It is already a feeling of confusion and chaos when it comes to AI usage such as gadgets and digital in this world, the information surge that too much information we can't handle. The future of medicine will change such as one of many examples' conversations between a doctor and their patient converting into a clinical summary. Is AI would know the difference between wrong and right information? (p.40). That is just one issue from that question. There will be more! We must remember that a human being thinks differently from an AI.

Artificial Intelligence is a programmed instrument. What that means is that AI has no common sense, conscience, and wisdom. No spiritual world that is. In every human being, there will always be a difference of thinking, understanding, and interpretation from the real mind, not from a program instrument like AI. A program instrument is programmed by a human being or shall I say 1 or 5 humans' thoughts from a human being, us. Each one of us as humans has many different *thoughts* within our real minds, the spiritual world that are programmed through *common senses, consciences, and wisdom.* Artificial Intelligence *is* ARTIFICIAL, and it is fake and programmed by human beings, NOT the spiritual world.

Chapter 9

Religions And The Humans In Our Society

In Time Magazine I read "Heaven, And the After Life, What's Awaits Us" explained the many types of religions and beliefs. Let us define one at a time of those beliefs. First, I believe in God, and I have a group of more than 500 members. I called this group "Sofia's Prayer Is Powerful Group." Within this group of Sofia's Prayer Is Powerful Group, there are five team groups, or shall I say a group that also has their own many members. My husband and I read prayer books, and read them every morning and share to our members. It is a way on digging in through the spiritual world, the unseen world on earth.

These prayer books I chose to buy focus on within us and our action here on earth, not a fantasy, not an imagination, but a real thing about ourselves, and our action here on earth, as the world have mixed with many unstable beliefs, and unstable rules and regulations. We must examine our actions here in this world of good and evil mixed, a very confusing world we are living in. It could be very hard to understand the usage of each word we as society is using.

Because the WORDS in this generation or perhaps from previous ones, words are changed, misused, and misunderstood. Therefore, confusion begins in each one of us. In the 21st Century, our dictionary, and Bible contents are changing. Previously, the meaning of Cult is a group of people getting together and create a business or Bible study together. Today, this is the meaning of the world "cult." "A cult is a small religious group that is not part of a larger and more accepted religion and that has beliefs regarded by many people as extreme or dangerous" (Google Dictionary, 2024). Let me tell you about my "Prayer Is Powerful" group.

I have more than 500 members now. I started with only 5 members. Am I a cult as what the meaning of today differs previously. Sharing our prayer every morning to all members helps us all. I have always mentioned in my writing that WORD is always a powerful tool in this world of very chaotic world of ours. I share the book of prayers my husband and I read every morning, and we pray. Sharing what we were reading to our members help our members to see themselves and God we called and guide their consciences and to come to light when there are disturbances within their minds and hearts while walking and journeying here on earth of plenty and abundance.

Every word what we say to release from our mouth is very meaningful and important to always watch it on how we say it, and on how we release it, because it affects someone's mind, and heart.

Similarly, in the book of mine the Two Universes of Self, understanding the self, physics, and the thought of ours also a good book to read. To process the understanding of self is to see and think what we say, release, and what we collected and accumulated within us, and gathered within our thought universe that affect the physic and the self which also affect the people around you. However, these days we have a very confusing world that affects every one of us, and those who we influenced and follow us as their guides in life.

Recently, we just heard about Artificial Intelligent and we as the society will be following AI and be our guide, therefore, it will be a very chaotic world added to already our leaders are being lost in this generation. What's going on once we are all managed by Artificial Intelligence? What our children going to become soon? Without using our real common sense, consciences, and wisdom, I said "REAL" not artificial that the Lord has given to all humanity since when we were born, what is next to happen to all the people on earth?

According to the Time Magazine I read, *"His work has potentially hastened the future he fears, in which AI becomes superhuman with disastrous results"* (Hinton, 2023, page 25*)*. Have you noticed that we are already here in this type of lifestyle, the AI phenomenon? It's getting and ingraining within us slowly, but very effectively. We must watch out for what we are doing while using our gadgets. Our information is gathered in the cloud, and companies have it all for instance when we book for hotels, and any type of vacation activities you may do are now using gadgets and seeking confidential information that is.

In religion, is AI going to be our interpreter, and as if AI has common sense, conscience, and wisdom like humans? Religions were made and programmed by humans anyway. However, is religion will be handled by AI? Do these AI creators truly understand the outcome of Artificial Intelligence? "Artificial" means it is not REAL, as I mentioned the meaning of CULT. Cult word is not a bad word, but we as humans interpret as a bad word. Again, the beginning of this passage, I have given you the meaning of cult. So, soon, AI will be guiding us, or shall we agree with that idea?

So, therefore, AI might be a cult. What are the consequences, and what are the benefits of having AI in our world of humans? What's going to happen to HUMANS' ability with ingrained knowledge through neurons and veins, such as having common sense, conscience, and wisdom? Does AI have those? Also, are religious teachings changing these days? The interpretations of God may not be the same when AI handles these types of beliefs. What do you think?

Chapter 10

Drugs/Medication/Alcohol/Food We Eat Everyday

Prescription drugs these days are continuing to be prescribed although not needed. Is AI has been used in this type of human activity, the reactivator in renewing prescription drug? Let me tell you about my experiences of prescription drugs when I was diagnosed of type 2 diabetes. I was told to take many medications, so I quit, and the result was amazing. For example, I was supposed to take metformin twice a day, and I doubted the ability of metformin due to there were times, it didn't work. I called my doctor and told him about my blood sugar is very high.

My doctor told me to take Januvia. The result was higher than it was. Therefore, my doctor said to discontinue Januvia. Then, I continued my metformin. I have been tested myself on eating vegetables such as broccoli, greens, avocado, and egg, and meat my sugar went down significantly. I do believe that doctors doing a routine job by what I called "Next" to line up patients in their clinic. Are our doctors of today using good common sense, and conscience?

To continue my experiences, I then discontinue my metformin one tablet at a time. It works. I was just wondering why doctors prescribed medication for only temporary results but also, medication gives more diseases such as side effects. Finally, I removed metformin, followed by removing lisinopril, and simvastatin soon. I have many medications left over, and of course, my insurance is paying for them, but I pay my insurance through my social security money.

This story of mine is just one of the many examples out there that do not make sense at all. I then dropped off my extra not used medications in the box outside the sheriff's office in the town I was living in. What a waste of money from my social security money from every retiree or anyone, such as health insurance, companies who are paying their employees, and individuals who are paying their prescriptions.

Besides, those people who uses drugs to make money like selling their own left-over prescription to anyone that is interested. I do remember, one of my tenants in my rental unit unable to pay her rent would sell her pain killer drugs to someone who is in pain. That is a very odd activity that no one knows in the health care industry, or shall I say we ignored all these odd actions by society because no one care? There are more about drugs and its usage that most health care industries know, the doctors, and in health care facilities. But it has been ignored.

Therefore, we have so many people on drugs in this country or in any other country we just do not know. The point I am making is that in the previous feudalistic era, people lived with the king in his compound, and everything was provided. Therefore, the provision was just enough for the things they needed. In this era, previously, and in this 21st Century is totally different. Not that we would like to go back to live at the King's Compound, but my point of view is our given freedom is taken advantage of by our society, the people, us.

In addition, alcohol is out there, ready to be purchased and be drunk until losing consciousness. Always taken advantage of the freedom we have and go our way, way, far that ruins ourselves as being alcoholic and drug addicted. Why? Too much freedom and ignored activities that are hidden from the public. Our children will grow up in that category and there are no rules and regulations anymore. It is a mentality of "Let It Be."

Therefore, people are so proud of being drunk and raise their glasses for a celebration of being drunkard. You will see those people who consume too much alcohol; they look old, and their skin is unhealthy looking. Their brains are not functioning in a healthy manner. We have an AA program, yes, we do, but we continue to advertise out there about wine drinking and using wine or alcohol to enjoy life. There are consequences of using alcohol as a tool to enjoy life.

Raise your glass and be glad today and tomorrow and near future. You will be a mess and lost in this world. What's going on with our food supply these days? Everything is processed and made up. Are we aware of that type of activity created by humans and then processed through AI? Every time I read the food information these days, I see and read that all foods are bad for our health. Examples are pesticides used, chemicals used for preservatives, food losing vitamins when it's too cooked, and much, much more information that is very confusing and does not make sense anymore. What's going to happen soon if AI rules the world? Is it here already?

In addition, what's going on in our food industry is too many chemicals in every food we eat. Therefore, we always get sick, and here comes the healthcare industry trying to rescue humans. Are they really trying to rescue humans and the sick? Many questions in our minds that there are no answers to because we trusted our government, the FDA, and many others that supposedly govern society for society's benefit for their own good only, but instead for the businesses and commercialization process for the benefit of the businesses, but ruins the societies to be healthy therefore, it will be costly for us all.

Chapter 11

The King's Compound VS. The Government System Rules and Regulations In Protecting the Society.

What is the meaning of the **feudal system**? According to Wikipedia (2023), the Feudal System is a combination of legal, economic, military, cultural, and political customs. Between the 9th and 15th centuries, this practice was very popular in medieval Europe. Although the word "Feudal" was derived from the Latin word Feodum or feudum and was used in the Medieval period, the term feudalism and the system. However, these practices were not a formal political system for the people who lived during the Middle Ages (Wikipedia 2023).

Thus, as I mentioned in previous chapters of feudalistic society in the 21st century, how do we, as real humans, live in this era? We, as humans in this era of feudalism, became the tools of experimentation for creating AI, and not just AI is used, but humans are used as experimentation, such as food, drugs and more! As mentioned, a long time ago, people lived in the king's compound. People's needs are provided by the king, such as food and shelter. However, there was no "salary" for the people who worked for the king in those past eras. Today, people work eight hours a day or more and must pay sales tax, and property tax and file income tax returns. Let us define what people are paying these days, how, why, and what causes them to go this far in consumerism behavior to boost the economy. In addition, we are the experimentation tools for creating AI.

It seems like we are still living in the compound of the king, but we must work hard to earn income, and you are paying the King instead now, not anymore that the King feeds and provides shelter for you. It is you who is paying the King, and the king pays the new entrants' people in this country, the land of the free. What can we do as we, the people supposedly having freedom, we call it in this new trend of the Feudalistic Era in the 21st Century?

In addition, the transhumanism development of this world, are humans, the real humans I would say, are we be able to survive when we do not exercise our naturally God given talents, and self-power as our capability to survive in this world, the human power, not the pro humans made by humans, us. Godly made versus humanly made which one is more durable, and lifetime existence of humans to exist here on the earth of plenty and abundance? It is coming that Artificial Intelligence (AI) is now becoming us. AI makers taking over our God given creativity, knowledge, and capabilities.

What's in your mind and heart matters may no longer exist in our society today. Bad guys are now protected but the good guys are not. What's going on in our society today. After the collapse of the Roman Empire, the feudalism era started. Society was looking for protection.

Society turns to kings and nobles. *"The king would grant land to nobles, the nobles would agree to fight for the king should the need arise, and the people would work the land and be under the protection of the kings and nobles"* (eNotes Editorial, 23 July 2013). However, there is no salary for these people who are under and living in the compound of the king. The crime begins when the legions withdraw and the empire crumbles. Lawlessness has grown and been overtaken both by the Vikings and the criminals. Thus, the lawlessness of the group of people could not prosper for long due to the economy collapsing when crops and farming were no longer functioning. Therefore, in that era a new system (*eNotes Editorial*, 23 July 2013).

In comparison, in today's 21st century, do you think we are lawless, the government crumbles, and many citizens are looking for protection in our society today? We only heard in the news about the disagreements in almost everything in the Whitehouse, and there has been so much chaos all over since COVID-19 announced, and more crumbles are coming due to the economy is heading to fall. People are looking for protection, one of many examples being the "Black Lives Matter." Now, I believe that the silent culture since then is the White. My own experiences as a Guardian Ad Litem volunteer, visiting the children that are with GALP, mostly are White blonde children.

These cultures of White people are now in the lower end of the society. As I mentioned in my other book, there should be no skin color, and culture identification once a person is categorized as an American Citizen, whether white, black, brown, yellow, and or tan color. Witnessing so many papers or documents to fill out, such as in a doctor's office and many others, the identification of one individual is digging deeper into where she or he came from, identifying through cultures and skin color. This type of documentation is also one of the many reasons we are very disunited in this country. Let me ask you this, "In this next generation, do you think our grandchildren and great-grandchildren will be the next to live in the King's Compound?"

What is contemporary feudalistic society? I have witnessed our society today as a signing agent for mortgages, and I am so surprised and so alarmed at how our society could ever survive feudalistic society then and at the present times. In those days when the people were the king's slave families lived in the King's compound and worked for the king for food and shelter. No salary since then. Our society still carries on the same legacy of the feudalistic society these days but in a different form. As our society is getting bigger and larger our responsibility in carrying the legacy of feudalism continues.

Just to name a few such as property taxes we continuously pay every year, sales tax, home insurance, car insurance and many kinds of type of insurance that include every purchase we make to feed our family, and everything we buy inserted some kind of taxes that goes to an entity to pay the piper. And the cost is getting higher and overwhelming for most of us. Most of it all is our health care industry on how to take care of our loved ones and the sick. That includes many different types of insurance, you name it. It's out there and pay attention to what you are paying these days.

Furthermore, in selling the idea of fears and worries for a pitch to promote products and services such as health insurance, many types of insurances the selling point will be to protect you and your family. But is it really? And you know what I mean. We can talk about everything I have mentioned, but I will focus on these issues in my other books in the near future titled "The Money Game." The Money Game book is a book that focuses on real estate property mortgage on what you are paying in buying a home for your family, including homeowner's insurance, flood insurance, property tax, interests, fees, fees, fees, and more fees. We have thought that when we bought a real estate property, we owned it and truly we have our own to call home instead of living in the compound being a slave by the king.

Realistically and philosophically, think for a second. We are still a slave of the king, which we now call the government system. By the time you really own your home, you pay off all your mortgages, which include fees and more fees, of course, plus interests. I would say, you do not own your home, and you are just the carrier and caretaker of property taxes, insurance, and many more. Therefore, why are we trying to be a homeowner if we do not really own your home? Think for a moment and check what you are paying.

Having a house to live in is just an illusion. However, if a person is smart enough to play the game of money, then it could be profitable. I will explain how to play the game of money as most investors do, and of course Uncle Sam. Because if you think about it, you are paying a mortgage every month plus interest, and truly Uncle Sam, the bank or mortgage companies, owned it, or shall we call it a "Lien Holder" to make it sound cool and to be blinded. You are just holding it to take care of that property for maintenance, property taxes, homeowner's insurance for the sake of your lien holder, and many, many more, and you are living in it, but you are paying for it plus you are responsible for taking good care of that property.

Crazy as it may sound, but that's the reality of this world as a homeowner or a caretaker of your property. Unless you live with the king in his compound in 300 BC, though! However, no salary, and you will work so hard to earn that free shelter and food. In previous centuries and in the present time, the 21st feudalistic century, you are just the caretaker of your own home, and I would say you are not the owner yet until you pay off your mortgage and remove the first lien holder of your property. You must take good care of the house and do some renovation or some maintenance for the sake of the living situation in that property. Plus, if you don't take care of the house, you will lose the value of your property, then your paid principal will not be recovered.

Your situation may be different from one another's life experiences, but you are still a taxpayer no matter what, and of course, that's *costly*. Do all human beings know how to play the Money Game? Look around you, and you will see many tiny houses, vans, RVs, and living in rundown mobile homes situated on a piece of land or lot. Living in this type of situation is invisible to most of us, but they are there living with children in slummy ground with no water and sewer because it is so costly to live a decent life. There are many other types of lifestyles that will not bring you to the disastrous type of lifestyle. Those are the ones that have no mortgage and credit card lifestyles and live a good life in the land of plenty and free.

In order for you to believe and be proud of yourself, you, as the so-called "Homeowner," take good care of it, and the exchange is what they call legal documents. You signed such documents to prove to the crowd or society that you own the property, but if you think about it, if you have a mortgage, you are the caretaker of that property for the investor, the mortgage company, or shall I call it "The Lien Holder." Does that sound better? Do you understand what I am saying? Let us compare the Feudalism era in the first century to perhaps the 15th century.

In the feudalism era, you were only to work for the king, and you would be fed, and the king provided food and shelter for you and your family. However, while working with the king, you do not have a salary. Therefore, you do not have expenses because the king pays for everything. You and your family are supposed to live at the King's compound and you do not pay for food and shelter, but you worked for the king without salary, so you are living for free. Thus, when freedom hits the minds of people, then revolt comes through, and people want freedom. Meaning that they want to get out of the King's compound, and they will work hard to get money for their family to be independent. Here we are today, people with *freedom*. The word Freedom today is misunderstood by many. Although there are changes along the way, it never gets easy.

So, you are looking for a house to buy with a white picket fence, and you've signed a contract, and your name is on the paper. Yes. I agree, but you will keep paying for it for life unless you have cash to pay it off. Do you? Then, you will borrow from your house, and we call it an Equity Line of Credit (ELC). More owed money to keep you paying your mortgage, property taxes, and many types of insurance. Therefore, would you agree with me that while you are still living, you are just a caretaker of that property, or shall I say, a real estate investment you may have? So, what's the difference between real estate investment and the home you are living in?

Let us clarify: we will separate your so-called real estate investment from yours versus the bank or mortgage investments. Think deeply. Open your eyes and rethink what you are paying for your property tax, homeowner's insurance and other fees, electricity, water, garbage disposal, and sewer. Put that together, you worked and pay for those fees. Every state or where you live carries a different amount of property tax you pay. Let's say $200,000.00 for a thirty-year mortgage you are paying your home $2,000.00 a month. This does not include property tax and other fees mentioned above. For example, you are paying your monthly mortgage of $2,300.00, including interest.

Well, you have paid the interest, too, that's how the mortgage companies earn their dollars. You must be working in order for you to pay those expenses and for your food. Your salary, for instance, is $4,000 a month. That $4,000 a month you must pay income tax. For instance, your net income would be $3,700.00, and you minus net income of $3,700-2,300 (monthly mortgage and interest payment) =$1,400.00 left over for groceries and other expenses such as property tax, homeowner's insurance, food, utility bills and other expenses such as gas for your car to go to work. I understand that you have 30 years to pay for your mortgage, but you are paying interest, too. So, you are young, and you still live 30 years or more and paid off your mortgage for 30 years and you are now 57 years old at almost retirement age. Do you know that you will continue paying your home property tax and insurance on your property while you are living in it until you die?

You cannot get out of that because first, you fear that your house might be hit by a tornado, and Uncle Sam wants part of it too. Therefore, you must continue paying property tax and home insurance. You cannot get out of it. You are still a slave, but yes, your name is on it to make you feel good about yourself and that you have accomplished something. In the feudalistic era, you did not have a document signed by you that you owned that property, but the king was the owner of the property you were living in. Contemporary feudalism is that you are awarded responsibilities, plus you are paying for it and give you more responsibilities because we as a society want it. We asked for freedom!

Another area where freedom is convoluted meaning is just like when you volunteer and work for free, and they get your gut to make you feel good. It is a similar situation. Just like those people were selling insurance and giving you a scenario just in case someone stole your TV, and if you are carried away by the calamity, insurance companies would be proud to explain all these fears that they put on your head so you buy for the cause of fear. Here is another popular activity of collecting money for free, donation. You name it, donation, donation the company would like to get free money from you. What they do is show you how other people suffer and are neglected, and it makes you sad and distressed that there are other people suffering, and you didn't even notice yourself suffering too due to other responsibilities you are carrying. You do not need to donate, but it gives you a distressing feeling of too much suffering somewhere. You are sold. You donate.

But the money you just donated is the salary for those donation collectors. These organizations that claim to be compiled with society's suffering say they are nonprofit and misunderstand the word "nonprofit" as truly this is how they profit from you. They get into your heart in a compelling way, so you won't be able to sleep that night when you see children starved and neglected. You will feel guilty, and you decide to give in. These charitable companies were able to do fundraising, but if they could get free money without hard work, why would they fundraise for the cause when they could just ask for money from society? Let me give you an example.

I am a fine artist and I used to have an art gallery and display artists' beautiful artwork. I have noticed that some art galleries or nonprofit organizations rely on grants to function in society. Nonprofit organizations and their members and volunteers have the opportunity and should have the ability to do fundraising through activities that create and produce cash. It just needs programming and hard work to fulfill.

However, most nonprofits are too lazy to do hard work jobs such as fundraising but only rely on scare tactics and advertise for humanity to be sad to psychologically get in their hearts and minds through manipulation of guiltiness to make you donate or give to their goals of getting your attention in a way to makes you give your cash for purpose, they say.

Do not get me wrong! In this contemporary feudalistic society, we are so blinded. Yes, disasters happen sometimes in our lifetime, but very few. Maybe disaster happens due to some created manipulation of the weather to create hurricane or rain? That's another study to really see to it how this happened. However, it is your choice where to live where there is no or less calamity, and you choose anyway where you want to live. So there! You pay. Where do you think that money goes when you pay your insurance company? It goes to the people affected by fear and that fear became true.

The money you pay for insurance goes to the people who are affected by weather or disastrous calamity. If you are not hit by these calamities, then you do not get paid. But your money goes to those who were affected by the calamities. So, some mentality says it's better to be affected by the calamities. Are we able to read their minds? Thus, whether this fear they caused and was caused by your imagination and acted upon it. It does not matter. They took you there. That's how our society is running, and of who we are as part of the clown we are participating in.

CONCLUSION

In the King's Compound eras, society relies on the king to provide food and shelter. In today's society, we work hard to provide for our necessities. However, commercialization and scare tactic makes us more vulnerable to too many expenses, and salary of the workers are just not enough to cover expenses. Scare tactics in marketing and other manipulations of the process for the people in business to earn income also have so many issues due to our products coming from other countries.

Therefore, many companies are merging and creating something new to cut down expenses, such as Artificial Intelligence products. However, AI has and will have consequences later once it is incorporated into our everyday activities. Our systems are changing and will affect us all. The bank systems are changing and there are companies and individuals who will be affected by these changes in the world. It is worrisome to most of us. We, as humans, we will be paralyzed. Why? Because our talents, creativity and productivity behavior will be lost, and we will become like zombies.

In today's era, we are very independent from the king in many different forms: plus, you must work, or some don't work. Must have a program for these people to go back to work to pay the piper. Most of our society today transformed into each one of us must work, but not all. Our digital world is changing to the extreme every year. We always have changes in our cell phone styles and more.

Not only cell phones but everything we need in this world, there always be a new gadget, and or updated function of all computers and gadgets. Artificial Intelligence is, or shall I say, taking over humanity's skills that could damage humans' capabilities to function. It is too fast that some people are unable to catch up. Therefore, as mentioned, the meaning of the feudalistic system is a Feudal System, a combination of legal, economic, military, cultural, and political customs. This practice was popular in the 9th and 15th centuries the medieval Europe. The economy is in chaos. Therefore, rules and regulations may change. Are we ready?

As we remember, a long time ago, people lived in the king's compound. The king provided food and shelter for the people but no "salary" for the people who worked for the king. We worked so much today, but it's going to change because AI will replace humans' creativity and productivity. Therefore, humans' capabilities will disappear soon. Perhaps it's already here! Do you feel it? Are we going to pay taxes on everything since our responsibility is given to the AI?

It seems like we are still living in the compound of the king, but we must work hard to earn income, and you are paying the King instead now, not anymore that the King feeds and provides shelter for you. It is you who is paying the King, and the king pays the new entrants' people in this country, the land of the free. By the way, the king owes more than thirty-four trillion dollars to the Federal Reserve. Why? Who will pay this debt the king owed? What should we do as we, the people supposedly having freedom, we call it in this new trend of the Feudalistic Era in the 21st Century? (www.bing.com/us.debt).

The End.

REFERENCES

Borden, K.S., and Abbott, B.B. (2008). Research design and methods: The process approach. New York, NY: McGraw-Hill Companies, Inc.

Bryman, A. (2004). Qualitative research on leadership: A critical but appreciative review. (Electronic version). *The Journal of Leadership Quarterly, 15, 729-769.*

Creswell, J.W., (2007). Qualitative inquiry and research design: Choosing among five approaches. Thousand Oaks, CA: Sage Publications.

Creswell, J.W., (2009). Research design: Qualitative, quantitative, and mixed methods approach. Los Angeles, CA: Sage Publications.

Dictionary, Google 2024, www.bing.com

Early Childhood Journal (2002). Editorial: On behalf of children. (Electron version). *The Journal of Early Childhood, 29-4, 217. eNotes Editorial,* 23 July 2013) https://www.enotes.com/homework-help/how-and-hy-did-feudalism-begin-444503. Accessed 17 May 2021).

Harari, Yuval Noah, Artificial Intelligence, 2023

Gibbon, P. H., (2001). The end of admiration. (Electronic version). Retrieved January 19, 2009 from http://www.meridianmagazine.com/ideas/011227admire.html.

+ Mertens, D.M. (2005). Research and evaluation in education and psychology: Integrating diversity with quantitative, qualitative, and mixed methods. Thousand Oaks, CA: Sage Publications, Inc.

+ Neuman, W. L. (2000). Social research methods, (4th edition) Boston, MA: Pearson Education, Inc.

+ Potter, G., (1998). Collaborative critical reflection and interpretation in qualitative research. (Electronic version). *Journal of Institute of Early Childhood and Family Studies, nv, 1-25.*

+ Ramsey, D. 2010). The Money Answer Book: Quick answer for your everyday financial question. Nashville, TN: Thomas Nelson.

+ Saiya, V.F., (2009). Who's raising our children? (Electronic version). Retrieved January 19, 2009 from http://georgiafamily.com/parenting_issues/who_raising_your_children.shtml

+ The Times Advertiser Magazine 2023 by Hinton.

About The Author

Sofia Laurden-Davis Adams is a PhD in Human Services specialized in Management in Nonprofit Agencies and Leadership graduated in April 2014 at Capella University. Dr. Adams is currently an Independent Contractor with mortgage, bank, law, and title companies function as a Certified Signing Specialist. Dr. Adams was born in Bohol Island Philippines. She came to United States in year 1984. She has 2 sons, Rhoss (Junjun) 41, and Danny (Jr) 34 years of age. Both sons are married, and currently she has six grandchildren. Danny is a medical doctor, and Rhoss is in logistics.

Since 1989, Dr. Sofia Laurden-Davis Adams worked in banking and real estate industries. At the beginning of the year 2000, she became an Independent Contractor working part time while pursuing her education. Currently, she is an entrepreneur, a volunteer of Guardian Ad Litem, serving as the voice for neglected and abused children in three counties in Panhandle Florida. and she taught 4th & 5th religious education in the church she attended. She teaches art classes and offers and she travels to art students' selected location. She is an Independent Contractor performing signings for mortgage, bank, and title companies.

Dr. Adams graduated as a Doctor of Philosophy (PhD) in April 2014. In 2006 she graduated with a master's degree in human resource management from the University of Phoenix. She has a bachelor's degree major in Art History, and Studio Art at Georgian Court University in New Jersey graduated in 2004, and an associate degree in liberal arts doubled with Photography at Brookdale Community College graduated in 2000. She moved from Bricktown, New Jersey to Bonifay Florida in 2004.

The same year, she developed a 501 C3 organization named Bonifay Guild for the Arts, Inc. which in year 2010 this organization was renamed to Laurden-Davis & Associates sole proprietorship consists of Mobile Signing Agent, Notary Public, Fine Art Studio, Online Art Gallery, and Rental Properties. Dr. Adams developed a yearbook for her previous organization titled, "Memorable Moments of Bonifay Guild for the Arts, Inc. Part 1" The book has 110 pages of compiled photos, stories, and activities of Bonifay Guild for the Arts, Inc. The yearbook copies were placed at Chambers of Commerce, and libraries for previous BGA and LDA members' keepsakes.

Dr. Sofia Laurden-Davis Adams and her husband Cameron plan to travel internationally. She plans to continue writing books and curricula, and as an independent contractor function as art teacher, Certified Signing Specialist. Dr. Adams published her books since year 2014 to this day. Check her books below:

www.authordrsofiaadams.com

www.amazon.com

www.ingramSpark.com

www.drsofiaadams.com

www.xlibris.com

www.iUniverse.com

www.morebooks.de

www.cameron-adams.com (and her husband Cameron is also an artist doing wood artworks.)